BREAD for WORDS

⤖A FREDERICK DOUGLASS STORY⤖

WRITTEN BY SHANA KELLER • ILLUSTRATED BY KAYLA STARK

I know where I was born, not when. It was Tuckahoe, Maryland.

I lived free as a bird near the bay in a small cabin with Grandma.
There wasn't a whole lot to do inside our cramped cabin, so I called to
the birds, the frogs, the cats, and the dogs. I chirped and barked and
squabbled until even the animals couldn't tell if I was one of their own.

One day, Grandma told me I would have to leave.

"Why?" I asked.

"We belong to Old Master," she said. "We are slaves."

"What does that mean?" I thought I belonged to Grandma.

"They won't teach you a thing, but to work.
And you won't have a choice."

"But **why am I a slave?**" I did not want to be told when to work,
where to work,
how to work . . .
and not have a choice.

Grandma was silent on the day we left the cabin early in the morning. We walked twelve long miles on a day swamped with heat and bugs to a place called the Great House Farm.

When we arrived, children ran out to see me. They surrounded me, laughing and teasing me so. Then Grandma left without saying goodbye. I met my brothers and sisters at the Great House, but I didn't know them well. Without Grandma, I was too sad to play.

Then I met Daniel; he lived in the Great House.

We hunted and hiked and fished together. Daniel occasionally
shared his cakes with me. He showed me the
Great House and all the grand rooms inside, including his.

Except for the color of our skin, it was hard to know
why we were different.

7

Daniel was not a slave. He wasn't born into it.

At night, Daniel slept in a warm bed with a full belly. **I had no bed.**

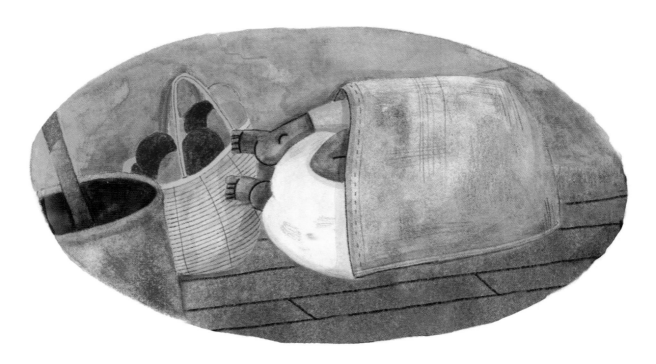

On the coldest nights, I slept with a bag used to carry corn.
It wasn't long enough to cover my feet, so I put it over my head.
I didn't have enough to eat or enough clothes to stay warm.

I didn't even know my age, but Daniel knew his.

When his tutor came, he taught Daniel to read and write and speak.

I wanted to learn, too, but Grandma was right. They didn't give me a choice.

I was not old enough to work in the field. I was told to clean the yards, keep the birds out of the garden, and drive the cows.

No matter how bad I wanted to learn to read and write,
they wouldn't teach me a thing. It was illegal, they said.

Unlawful.

Unsafe.

Why? I walked like them. I talked like them. I walked and talked exactly like them. I showed them I could.

Is that why I was sent to Baltimore, far away from my brothers and sisters?

I left the plantation the same way Grandma did, without saying goodbye.

In Baltimore, I lived with Mr. Hugh Auld, kin to Old Master, and his wife, Mrs. Sophia. **I was told to take care of little Thomas**, their young son.

City life was different from plantation life. There was plenty of food for me to eat, and warm clean clothes for me to wear. At night, **I now had a good straw bed, with covers**.

Mrs. Sophia was kind at first. She knew as little of slavery as I did. When she read to Thomas from the Bible, I followed along. To my surprise, she taught me what no one else would: my ABCs.

She taught me how to spell next. I felt proud to know three- and four-letter words. She was proud of me, too. But when Mr. Auld saw what I could do, anger caught ahold of him.

"He **should know nothing, but to do as he is told**," he said. "If you teach Freddy how to read, **there would be no keeping him**."

He forbade Mrs. Sophia from teaching me.

From that moment, I understood the pathway from slavery to freedom. If I learned to read, I could loosen the chains of bondage.

I couldn't give up, but how would I learn now that I had lost my teacher?

As Thomas grew older, I was told to carry his books and walk him to school.

An idea came to me.

I met a lot of hungry boys on the streets.

The boys were between nine and twelve years old.
Was I as old as them?

I remembered how I hated the **pinches** of hunger in my belly. This time, my hunger was different from theirs. **When I was sent on errands, I always took my book with me** and I took extra bread.

When I saw the boys on the streets, I offered them bread for words.

It worked! With their help, **at different times and in different places**, I finally learned to read.

But to break free from slavery, I knew I had to learn how to write next. A new idea came to me in the shipyard.

I watched the ship carpenters carve letters into pieces of wood to show which part of the ship it would be used for. **I soon learned the names of these letters.** They carved *L* for *larboard*, or left side; *F* for *forward*; *S* for *starboard*, the right side; and *A* for *aft*, the stern.

With a lump of chalk, I wrote on fences, brick walls, and pavement.

I copied these **four letters** until I could write them from memory.

25

To learn the rest of the alphabet, I challenged those boys on the street who I knew could write. I said **I could write** as well as them.

They didn't believe me.

I carefully wrote the letters I had practiced.

Beat that.

Unable to resist my game, they wrote the letters they knew.

I paid close attention to the ones I didn't.

At home, when Thomas finished with his copybooks, they were set aside
and forgotten. I used the books to trace the letters again and again
until I could make them all without looking at the books.

After nearly seven years,
I finally succeeded in learning
how to read and write.

Mr. Auld was right.
There would be no keeping me.
My chains had been broken.

Frederick Douglass — His Life

In 1818, Frederick Augustus Washington Bailey, who later in life changed his name to Frederick Douglass to avoid capture, was born enslaved in Talbot County, Maryland.

When he was nearly six years old, Frederick, like his kin before him, was sent to live and work at the Wye Plantation (also called the Great House Farm or Wye House), a massive enterprise owned by Colonel Edward Lloyd. Colonel Lloyd employed Aaron Anthony, the head overseer, who enslaved Frederick and his family.

On the Wye Plantation, Frederick witnessed and experienced physical abuse, neglect, and humiliation. Children had little more than shirts to wear. Even the knowledge of their age and birth date was kept from them. Amid this misery, Frederick met Daniel, one of Colonel Lloyd's sons. Daniel took Douglass under his wing and at times shared his food with him. Frederick found another ally in Lucretia Anthony Auld, Aaron Anthony's daughter. Frederick ran errands for her. In return, she provided him with extra bread to eat. Several years after his arrival at the Wye Plantation, Frederick was sent to live and work for Lucretia's brother-in-law, Hugh Auld, and his wife, Sophia.

In Baltimore, Frederick's lifestyle drastically changed. Sophia introduced Frederick to reading. Charmed by his ability to spell three- and four-letter words, she had Frederick show his skills to her husband. Appalled, Hugh scolded his wife and inadvertently presented Frederick with his first antislavery speech. Sadly, Sophia turned against Frederick and opposed his education with more fervor than her husband.

Despite the dire warning and outright forbiddance from the Aulds, young Frederick, who yearned for freedom and understood "that education and slavery were incompatible with each other," continued his lessons. Unlike his previous home, the Aulds had plenty of food for Frederick to eat. No stranger to starvation, Frederick took bread with him on errands and offered it to the boys he met on the streets in

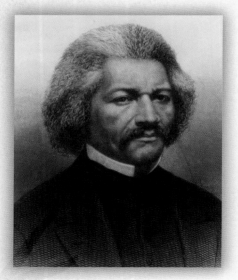

exchange for lessons. Once he mastered reading, Frederick played games that challenged the boys to write in front of him. He observed them carefully, memorizing their technique. It took him many years to learn, but he never gave up.

Several years after finally escaping to the north in 1838, Frederick lectured as an abolitionist. He wrote countless speeches, worked for antislavery papers before he started his own, and penned three autobiographies. Undeterred by assault, injury, or intimidation, Frederick Douglass became a magnificent orator, author, educator, and human right's activist. He died a free man in 1895.

Author's Note

As a child, I grew up with very little exposure to African American history. It wasn't until high school that I first learned about Frederick Douglass. As an adult, I revisited his life and was amazed by his tenacity to teach himself how to read and write, considering all the challenges he faced.

When crafting this story, it was important to me that young readers had access to Frederick's own words and that the overall events remained true to his descriptions. Frederick's full and partial quotes within the story are indicated in bold type, the majority of which come from his first autobiography, *Narrative of the Life of Frederick Douglass, an American Slave*.

Despite the discrepancies in his three autobiographies, I stuck as close to Frederick's ideology and terminology as possible while also considering questions children of that age and in that era would most likely have asked. Thus, I was inspired to write in first person, honoring the legacy of his autobiographies, and present his soulful question, "Why am I a slave?" early on in the story. It is also why I kept his verbiage intact when using the term *slave*, as Douglass did, rather than *enslaved*, as many historians and educators do today and rightfully so, as it demonstrates that slavery was enforced and not voluntary. At the end, I reused the powerful quote "There would be no keeping him" and exchanged the word *him* with *me* on page 29, to emphasize Frederick's determination and mark that moment as he did, as "a grand achievement," that set him on the path to freedom and the pursuit of equality.

NOTES

p. 3: "Why am I a slave?" Douglass, Frederick, *My Bondage and My Freedom* (New York: Miller, Orton & Mulligan, 1855), 89.

p. 8: "I had no bed." Douglass, Frederick, *Narrative of the Life of Frederick Douglass, an American Slave* (Boston: Anti-Slavery Office, 1845), 27.

p. 10: "I was not old enough to work in the field." Douglass, *Narrative of the Life of Frederick Douglass, an American Slave*, 26.

p. 11: "unlawful [. . .] unsafe . . ." Douglass, *Narrative of the Life of Frederick Douglass, an American Slave*, 33.

p. 14: "I was told to take care of little Thomas . . ." Douglass, *Narrative of the Life of Frederick Douglass, an American Slave*, 30.

p. 14: "I now had a good straw bed [. . .] with covers." Douglass, *My Bondage and My Freedom*, 144.

p. 16: "should know nothing but [. . .] to do as he is told..." Douglass, *Narrative of the Life of Frederick Douglass, an American Slave*, 33.

p. 16: "there would be no keeping him." Douglass, *Narrative of the Life of Frederick Douglass, an American Slave*, 33.

p. 17: "From that moment, I understood the pathway from slavery to freedom." Douglass, *Narrative of the Life of Frederick Douglass, an American Slave*, 33.

p. 20: "pinches . . ." Douglass, *My Bondage and My Freedom*, 75.

p. 20: "When I was sent [on] errands, I always took my book with me . . ." Douglass, *Narrative of the Life of Frederick Douglass, an American Slave*, 38.

p. 21: "at different times and in different places . . ." Douglass, *Narrative of the Life of Frederick Douglass, an American Slave*, 38.

p. 23: "I soon learned the names of these letters." Douglass, *Narrative of the Life of Frederick Douglass, an American Slave*, 43.

p. 25: "four letters . . ." Douglass, *Narrative of the Life of Frederick Douglass, an American Slave*, 43.

p. 26: "I could write . . ." Douglass, *Narrative of the Life of Frederick Douglass, an American Slave*, 43.

p. 27: "Beat that." Douglass, *Narrative of the Life of Frederick Douglass, an American Slave*, 43.

p. 28: "until I could make them all without looking . . ." Douglass, *Narrative of the Life of Frederick Douglass, an American Slave*, 44.

p. 29: "I finally succeeded in learning . . ." Douglass, *Narrative of the Life of Frederick Douglass, an American Slave*, 44.

p. 29: "There would be no keeping [me]." Douglass, *Narrative of the Life of Frederick Douglass, an American Slave*, 33.

SELECTED BIBLIOGRAPHY

Adler, David A. *Frederick Douglass: A Noble Life*. New York: Holiday House, 2010.

Blight, David W. *Frederick Douglass: Prophet of Freedom*. New York: Simon & Schuster, 2018.

Bontemps, Arna. *Frederick Douglass: Slave-Fighter-Freeman*. New York: Alfred A. Knopf, 1959.

Douglass, Frederick. *Life and Times of Frederick Douglass*. Hartford, CT: Park Publishing Co., 1882.

Douglass, Frederick. *My Bondage and My Freedom*. New York: Miller, Orton & Mulligan, 1855.

Douglass, Frederick. *Narrative of the Life of Frederick Douglass, an American Slave*. Boston: Anti-Slavery Office, 1845.

McCurdy, Michael; Edited and Illustrated. *Escape from Slavery: The Boyhood of Frederick Douglass in His Own Words*. New York: Alfred A. Knopf, 1994.

Archives, Newspapers, and Journals

Gregory, James M. *Frederick Douglass, The Orator*. Springfield, MA: Willey Co., 1893.

Perry, Patsy Brewington. "*Before The North Star: Frederick Douglass' Early Journalistic Career*." Clark Atlanta University: *Phylon*, vol. 35, no. 1 (1974), pp. 96–107.

The Ram's Horn. New York: Van Rensselaer & Hodges, 1847.

For Barb McNally,
thank you for helping me share my words.

—Shana

For Brad Henderson,
thank you for your many pep talks and endless patience.

—Kayla

ACKNOWLEDGMENTS

I'd like to thank Bradley Alston, Urban Ranger, the Baltimore National Heritage Area, and the Frederick Douglass-Isaac Myers Maritime Park and Museum/Living Classrooms-Baltimore, for taking the time to discuss all history related to Frederick Douglass. The tour, as well as Bradley's personal insight, proved invaluable. I'd also like to thank Shauntee Daniels, executive director of the Baltimore National Heritage Area (www.explorebaltimore.org), for introducing me to Mr. Alston. And finally, a special thanks to Kaili Lockbeam, registrar and collection manager, Reginald F. Lewis Museum, for answering my questions and sharing her love of history with me.

—Shana

SLEEPING BEAR PRESS™

2395 South Huron Parkway, Suite 200
Ann Arbor, MI 48104
www.sleepingbearpress.com

Printed and bound in the United States.

10 9 8 7 6 5 4 3 2 1

Library of Congress Cataloging-in-Publication Data

Names: Keller, Shana, 1977- author. | Stark, Kayla, illustrator.
Title: Bread for words / written by Shana Keller ;
illustrated by Kayla Stark.
Description: Ann Arbor, MI : Sleeping Bear Press, [2020]
| Audience: Ages 6-10 | Summary: "Frederick Douglass knew that learning to read and write would be the first step in his quest for freedom. Told from first-person perspective and using some of Douglass's own words, this biography draws from his experiences as a young boy and his attempts to learn how to read and write."— Provided by publisher.
Identifiers: LCCN 2019036853 | ISBN 9781534110014 (hardcover)
Subjects: LCSH: Douglass, Frederick, 1818-1895—Childhood and youth—Juvenile literature.
| Slaves—Maryland—Biography—Juvenile literature. | Slaves—Books and reading—Maryland—History—19th century—Juvenile literature. | Literacy—Maryland—History—19th century—Juvenile literature.
| Writing—Southern States—History—19th century—Juvenile literature. | Abolitionists—United States—Biography—Juvenile literature. | African American abolitionists—Biography—Juvenile literature.
Classification: LCC E449.D75 K45 2020 | DDC 973.8092 [B]—dc23
LC record available at https://lccn.loc.gov/2019036853

P 30 Frederick Douglass / engraved by A.H. Ritchie., 1868.
[Hartford, Conn.: Hartford Publishing Co] Photograph. https://www.loc.gov/item/2014645333/.